Gail the Snail

Written by
Debbie Strayer

Illustrations by
Joy Majewski

New Sounds:

sn

ai　　a_e　　ay

(Note: The pictures indicate the sound, not the spelling.)

Common Sense Press

© 1998 by Common Sense Press

Printed 09/15

8786 Highway 21 • Melrose, FL 32666

ISBN 1-880892-59-6

This is Gail the Snail.
She is on the trail. The
trail is by the lake.

What is in the way? It is Jake the Snake. He wants to play.

Jake will shake his tail. Gail may stay in her shell.

Jake will make a good playmate. They can sail on the lake.

They like to play all day.
They sail to the trail.

Gail wants to bake a cake. Jake will get the tray.

Jake put the cake on a plate. Gail will take it away.

It is late. Jake and Gail will play another day.

New Words:

ai	a_e	ay	sn
snail	lake	way	snail
trail	snake	play	snake
sail	shake	may	
tail	make	stay	
Gail	bake	day	
	cake	tray	
	take	away	
	plate	**play**mate	
	Jake		
	late		
	play**mate**		
	_____		
	shell		

New Sight Words:

wants   put   by   another   her   she

Review Words:

the	is	can	all	get	on
what	in	like	will	to	it
he	his	a	good	they	this